# HIELAND FOODIE

# HIELAND FOODIE

## A Scottish culinary voyage with Clarissa

Clarissa Dickson Wright with Henry Crichton-Stuart

**NMS Publishing**

Published by NMS Publishing Limited,
Royal Museum,
Chambers Street,
Edinburgh EH1 1JF

Details of other titles can be found at www.nms.ac.uk

British Library Cataloguing in Publication Data
A catalogue record of this book is
available from the British Library

ISBN 1 901663 07 8

Designed, created and produced
by Creative Imprint Ltd, Glasgow.

Printed and bound in Italy

# Contents

A culinary trip around
Scotland and through
Scotland's history
whimsically illustrated
with treasures from
the Museum
of Scotland...

We are the product of our genetic geographicals; my grandfather was a Glasgow doctor whose main aim, it seems to me, was to bring the preachings of the Plymouth Brethren to the poor of Govan, funded by his Helensburgh practice. My father told me colourful and probably exaggerated stories of his childhood in Glasgow with tales of the Mayfest and adventures on trams with his wild friends. He left, as so many did, for the Great War, and though fortunate enough to survive it, never returned to live here. My grandmother left Aberdeen for Australia in her teens. Scotland keeps a strong hold on the hearts of her children and no-one is more partisan than an expatriate Scot. Pipe Major Robertson played at my mother's graveside the lament he had promised; year after year my father dragged us up Goatfell on Arran in the rain. I was born and raised in England but such is the bondage of Gaeldom that I have never considered myself English.

Almost six years ago, on business with Henry Crichton-Stuart, I came to Scotland. It was not my intention to stay, but one day on the train crossing the Border I felt a great wave of 'isn't it lovely to be home', that I had never felt anywhere in my life. I had no money, and all my opportunities were in England. I made a pilgrimage to Dunfermline, threw myself on the mercy of St Margaret and stayed. The kindness of James Thompson, whose restaurant The Tower is in the Museum of Scotland paid my rent and for the rest I lived on air.

Scotland has been a kind home: I have many loved friends, I am Lord Rector of the ancient University of Aberdeen, I run the catering at Lennoxlove, family home of the country's premier Duke (my friend Angus Hamilton, whose wife's recipe for Rowies appears in this book), I am godmother to the Lord of the Isles, Godfrey Macdonald... Most of all I feel I am home.

Henry's cousin John, 6th Marquis of Bute, sadly never lived to see completion of his vision of the Museum of Scotland, and it was Henry who persuaded me into this book and Henry who bullied, kicked, cajoled and charmed me (with the charm only the Stuarts can produce) to finish it in a year so busy I never wish to see its like again. When I saw what Helen Kemp has done to produce it I fell in love with it as I hope you will.

Scotland has a strong food tradition and produces wonderful ingredients; it is a thrifty country and produces them carefully. Her coal gave her the edge on baking, and woe betide the Scots girl who cannot produce a good scone for her mother-in-law. The frying pan has been a poor friend to modern Scotland but no nutritionalist could fault the historic diet of oatmeal, oily fish and kail with haggis for highdays and a bit of beef, venison or mutton for holidays. You will find Scots' names on every battlefield or piece of engineering throughout the world, the energy of her children reflecting the quality of her food.

This book is by no means exhaustive. It is an amuse-guele to tempt you, and show you that our ancestors ate good and interesting food. I will leave it to the likes of Claire Macdonald, Sue Lawrence, Catherine Brown and the late great Marian MacNeill to fill in the main courses. It is a historic taster into which you can dip for a feel of the country through the ages, whether the high life of Mary Stuart, the simple croft, the Age of Enlightenment, or the deep-fried Mars Bar of today. The high teas of my youth have sadly disappeared; there are increasingly good restaurants, but when the only place recommended by the Inverness Tourist Guide is an Indian restaurant we have a way to go.

I hope you will enjoy my offering and cook the past – if you have problems with the haggis you can buy many good ones ready made! Some people think Scotland's food is largely the product of outside influences. I strongly disagree. The country opens itself to what incomers have to offer, but stamps its own inimitable mark, whether it be as terrifying as the haggis and doner kebab pizza or as delicious as the smoked haddock risotto they serve in the Tower. Have fun with this book and bear in mind that as the objects you see around you in the Museum of Scotland are often more beautiful, though produced with less technology, than things we make today, so our ancestors' food may have been more delicious than we might think.

*Clarissa Dickson Wright — June 1999*

# Potted Salmon

In the days before refrigeration it was necessary to preserve food by all manner of means. Potting (preserving the food by sealing it from the air with fat) is a remarkably successful and easy means of preserving, and indeed the food matures within the fat. Salmon was excessively plentiful in Scotland, but for a limited season only while the salmon were running upstream to spawn. Whilst you don't need this recipe as a preservative today (freezers and fish farms have seen to that) it is a delicious way of preparing farmed salmon (which can need a little help) and makes an excellent starter.

allspice

mace

peppercorns

slice of cold cooked salmon

3 whole anchovies

1/2 lb butter

1/2 tsp mace

salt and cayenne pepper

To cook salmon for potting, butter the inside of a crock, put in the fish and add powdered allspice, mace and peppercorns. Cook slowly for 1 hour, drain and cool.

Pound the anchovies in a mortar, add the salmon, seasonings and butter and pound well again. When it is all well pounded and mixed pass through a sieve. (This can all be done in a food processor.) Put in a lidded jar and pour melted butter over the top.

Donald MacDonald
of Arisaig with a
substantial catch,
photographed by
MEM Donaldson,
about 1910.

# POTTED CRAB

Crab is a great east coast delicacy, and one of the nicest ways
of preparing it is to add a little butter and nutmeg.

2 large cooked crabs

115g/4oz butter

nutmeg

1 lemon

salt and pepper

Remove the meat from the crabs, discarding dead men's
fingers. Melt the butter in a heavy pan
and add the crab meat, season with salt
and pepper and a good grating of
nutmeg and heat through. A few minutes
before serving add the lemon juice.

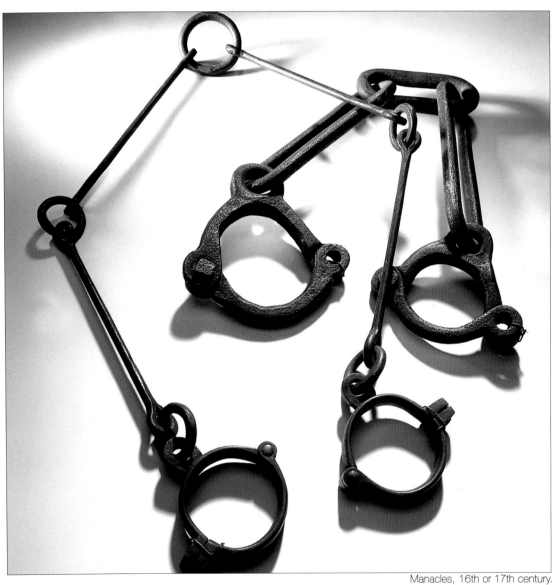

Manacles, 16th or 17th century.

# Mussel Brose

I live by the 'honest toun' of Musselburgh which stands on the
Firth of Forth east of Edinburgh. There is a huge mussel bed
here, harvested since Roman times. Sadly today the Forth is
too polluted to allow of their eating but I like to think of the
shades of the toun feasting on this very good broth.

600ml/1 pint mussels per person
150ml/ 1/4 pint fish stock per person
150ml/ 1/4 pint milk
1 tbsp oatmeal per person

Clean and wash the mussels well, put them over the heat in a
heavy pan until they open, remove them from their shells
reserving their liquor. Add the liquor to the fish stock and the
milk and bring to the boil. Add the mussels and cook for 10
minutes. Toast some oatmeal on a flat metal surface in the oven
and divide it among the serving bowls, ladle over the broth and
serve very hot.

Spoons made from cattle horn, 18th and 19th century.

## White Soup (serves 16)

The next three recipes, all variants on a theme, show the progression of this soup from robust to elegant. White soup is a traditional Scottish soup in a country which has a long and loving history of soup making: in its original version it still has a clean clear flavour and a certain elegance; in its second phase it comes under the influence of Mary of Guise, daughter of the Duke of Lorraine and mother of Mary Queen of Scots, and we see the use of ground almonds, egg yolks and cream as a thickening agent. In its third existence it becomes the 'Feather Fowlie' beloved of Mary, Queen of Scots herself and a dainty and refined dish. I can think of few examples where such a direct progression in a dish can be so readily traced.

| | |
|---|---|
| 1 knuckle of veal | 2 blades of mace |
| 1 boiling fowl | 1 sprig lemon thyme |
| 115g/4oz lean bacon | 12 white peppercorns |
| 85g/3oz each of carrots and onions | 4.2 litres/7 pints water |
| 225g/8oz turnips | salt and pepper |
| half head of celery | |

Chop all the vegetables, place all the ingredients in a large pan, bring to the boil and skim. Simmer gently for 2 hours skimming as necessary. Strain carefully. Cool, and when it is set remove surface fat and sediment, reheat and simmer for 30 minutes.

## Lorraine Soup

| | |
|---|---|
| 3 litres/5 pints white soup | 1 tsp grated nutmeg |
| 225g/8oz minced white chicken meat | 275g/10oz ground almonds |
| 55g/2oz white breadcrumbs | salt and pepper |
| 4 hard-boiled egg yolks | 750ml/1 1/4 pints double cream |

Mix together the egg yolks, chicken and breadcrumbs, nutmeg and lemon peel. Stir the ground almonds into the white soup and simmer for 20 minutes, add the chicken mixture and simmer for another 10 minutes. Adjust seasoning, add cream and heat through gently and serve.

## Feather Fowlie

Omit the veal when making the white soup, but add a faggot of
herbs and only simmer for 1 1/2 hours. Remove the best meat
from the chicken skin and mince finely.

2 egg yolks

150ml/5 fl oz cream

1 tbsp chopped parsley

When the soup is cooled and skimmed return
3 1/2 pints to a clean pan. Simmer for
20 minutes, then remove from
the heat. Blend the egg
yolks and the cream,
add to the soup and
heat through
without boiling,
stir in the
minced
chicken
and the
parsley.

Wemyss ware plate
made by Heron's Fife Pottery.

# Cullen Skink

Scotland has 167 types of smoked or cured haddock,

including some hung on the yards of fishing boats

to dry – how did they keep the gulls off?

Among the finest is the Findon

haddie, from the Moray Firth,

which is smoked on the bone.

This is a traditional soup, or skink, very comforting and

delicious.

a Findon haddock

1 onion

1/2 lb mashed potatoes

1 tbsp butter

black pepper

Skin the haddock, place in a pan and barely cover with boiling

water. Bring to the boil, chop the onion and add it. When the

haddock is cooked remove from the liquid and remove all its

bones. Return the bones to the stock and simmer for 1 hour.

Flake the fish and set aside. Strain the stock and bring it back

to the boil. In a separate pan boil a pint of milk and add it, with

the flaked fish, to the stock. Bring back to the boil, add enough

mashed potato to thicken the soup and the butter, season with

salt and pepper. Bring back to the boil and serve.

Goose and fish on a
Pictish Symbol stone
from Easterton of
Roseisle, Moray.
7th-8th century AD.

# Meg Merilees Soup

Meg Merilees was the gypsy girl in Sir Walter Scott's novel Guy
Mannering, and this is a reconstruction of her soup or stew. It
is, however, a typical game stew cooked in one pot which
would have been found in any rural Scots house during the
game season.

The varieties are infinite but the effect is very rich and satisfying.
For refinement the game can be removed from the bones
before serving but it is quite nice to sook on them.

1 brown hare cut in pieces

2 pheasants

2 partridges

2 grouse

4 onions

6 leeks

6 potatoes

flour

butter

salt and pepper

2.4 litres/4 pints water

Cut all the game into pieces and toss in seasoned flour. Heat
some butter and brown all the game pieces. Chop the onions
and leeks and colour them in the butter. Place everything
except the potatoes in a large pan with the water, bring to the
boil and simmer for 1 hour, add the potatoes roughly chopped
and cook for a further 1/2 hour.

19th-century
cast iron
cooking pots.

# Leeks and Beetroot in Raisin Sauce

Leeks grow particularly well in East Lothian and we know the Romans exported leeks from Scotland to Rome, along with Kelso onions and native oysters, where they were much prized. The Musselburgh leek so identified by the late Mr Scarlett is the dominant British leek and, as the Romans had substantial settlements in the area, it was probably the ancestor of the present leek that was so sought after. This recipe is a genuine Roman one from Apicius, the great gourmet who killed himself because he was down to his last million sesterces which would, he thought, pay only for one good party and that his funeral.

2 leeks, sliced
225g/8oz young whole beetroots
1 tsp coriander seeds
1/4 tsp cumin seeds
55g/2oz raisins
600ml/1 pint vegetable stock
olive oil
white wine vinegar
flour
salt

Grind together the cumin and coriander. Heat the stock and add the raisins and spices. Put in the vegetables, add salt and simmer until the vegetables are tender (about 25 minutes). Remove the vegetables from the sauce to a warm dish. Reduce the sauce, adding a little flour to thicken and a dash of oil and vinegar. Pour over vegetables and serve.

Part of the silver treasure from Traprain Law, East Lothian, about AD 400.

# Mushroom Pasties

Mushrooms abound in Scotland and, due no doubt to the French influence, were much more happily and widely eaten here than they were in England. This recipe for little mushroom pasties is a medieval dish and very good as a canape or for picnics.

450g/1lb shortcrust pastry
450g/1lb mushrooms
2 tbsp olive oil
2oz mature cheese, grated
salt
black pepper
mace
1 egg, beaten

Line small deep patty pans with two thirds of the pastry. Chill. Scald the mushrooms in boiling water for two minutes, dry and chop them. Mix with the oil, cheese and seasonings. Make lids with the remaining pastry. Fill the pasties and seal the lids with beaten egg. Make a hole in each and glaze with the remaining egg. Bake at 200C/400F/Gas 6 for 15 minutes or until golden.

17th-century German jug
found on the sea bed 70
miles east of Eyemouth,
Berwickshire.

# THE BUTT AND BEN'S ARBROATH CREPE

Scotland's great legacy to food is cold smoking of fish and, when it comes to haddock, ingenuity knows no bounds. There are at least 69 recorded variants on the theme including some which are sun-dried: a patient version with Scots weather! Everyone knows the Arbroath smokie and it is such an old product that it is nice to think that Robert I's stirring declaration of independence at Arbroath in 1320 might have been composed over a supper of them. What most people don't know, however, is that the Arbroath smokie originated along the coast to Auchmithie and only moved when the trade became too large. If you go to Auchmithie you must go to that excellent little restaurant the Butt and Ben, this delicious recipe is theirs.

FOR THE CREPE:

115g/4oz flour

pinch of baking powder

150ml/1/4 pint full-cream milk

1 egg

pinch of salt

FOR THE FILLING:

1 pair of smokies

55g/2 oz butter

300ml/1/2 pint double cream

Mix together the batter ingredients and leave to stand for 1 hour at least. Strip the flesh from the smokies and flake the meat. Heat in a pan the butter and cream to just below boiling point, throw in the flaked smokies and heat through. Make 4 crepes with the batter and divide the smokie mixture equally between them, fold over and pour over the remaining sauce. Serve on hot plates.

Preparations for white fishing, mainly for haddock and cod, in Auchmithie, Angus, around 1890. Scottish Life Archive

SHELLING THE MUSSELS, AUCHMITHIE.

# Tuppenny Struggles

I love the name of these little mutton pies but have found no reason for it, possibly the addition of the more expensive currants and fruit jelly may have raised the price to tuppence but I am still at a loss with 'Struggles'. Scotland has long been famous for its mutton pies, and each region produces its own variety. My brother-in-law, the artist Harry Moore-Gordon, frequently extols the pies he ate in Montrose during the war to the exception of all others. I imagine that rowan jelly would have been more traditional than redcurrant.

450g/1lb minced cooked mutton

340g/12oz hot water pastry

300ml/1/2 pint brown ale

salt and pepper

1 tsp vinegar

pinch nutmeg

1 tbsp currants

redcurrant jelly

sugar

Mould the pastry into six individual shapes about 8.5cm/3 1/2 inches wide and 3.5cm/1 1/2 inches high. Moisten the meat with the vinegar and brown ale. Season with salt and pepper and nutmeg and divide equally between the shells. Place a few currants, a pinch of sugar and a touch of redcurrant jelly on top of each, cover with pastry lids, make a hole in the top of each, brush with egg and bake at 180C/350F/Gas 4 for 40 minutes.

FOR THE PASTRY:

450g/1lb plain flour

1 1/2 tsp salt

115g/4oz lard

225ml/7fl oz water

Sift flour and salt into a large bowl. Heat the lard and water
gently in a saucepan until the lard melts then bring to the boil.
Make a well in the centre of the flour and quickly mix in the lard
and water to make a fairly soft dough. Turn onto a floured
surface and knead till smooth. Quickly use as required, keeping
the dough not in use covered and warm to prevent hardening.

Brae Moray Tup, 1845 by Gourlay Steell.

A portrait of one of the last Whiteface or Dunface sheep in Scotland, a medieval and prehistoric breed.

# Bacon Stovies

6-8 portions

The word 'stovie', describing a type of stew cooked on top of the stove, takes its name from the French 'estuvier' and is yet another instance of the lowland Scots adaption of French terms into the language. Other examples include 'I'm away the messages' (doing the shopping) from the French 'messuage' and giggit of lamb for a leg of lamb from 'gigot'. This bacon stovie is an inexpensive and comforting dish.

1.125kg/2 1/2 lb forehock bacon
450g/1lb chopped onions
900g/2lb sliced potatoes
dry mustard
pepper
1 bay leaf
milk

Cut the bacon into 2.5cm/1 inch cubes and arrange in alternate layers with the onions and potatoes in a pan. Sprinkle each layer with pepper and a little mustard, finishing with a layer of overlapping potatoes. Lay the bay leaf on the very top and pour over enough milk to come level with the top layer of potatoes. Cover with a lid and simmer gently for 1 1/2 to 2 hours.

Wemyss ware pig bank by Robert Heron & Sons, Fife Pottery, Kirkcaldy, late 19th century.

Native British oysters were particularly prized by the Romans.
The Emperor Nero boasted (he was prone to that particular vice
among many others) that he could tell by taste alone from what
part of his vast Empire any oyster came. The oysters were
transported in barrels, packed in seaweed, and continually
refreshed with seawater. The Romans were great fish eaters
and paid large sums of money for their favourite types: there is
a piece by the poet Juvenal touching on people wasting their
whole inheritance to purchase a prize fish. The Romans
esteemed the red mullet as much as their descendants do
today but they were also surprisingly fond of grey mullet, a fish
regularly found in Scottish waters.

8 fish fillets
6 oysters
150ml/1/4 pint fish stock
4 eggs
150ml/1/4 pint white wine
olive oil
black pepper

In a buttered dish bake your fish in a preheated oven at
180C/350F/Gas 4 for ten minutes. Remove and flake it back
into the dish in which it was cooked. In a sauce pan put 1/4
pint each of wine and fish stock and bring to the boil. Add two
tbsps olive oil and the juice of the oysters. Return to the boil,
add the oysters and heat through. Pour this sauce over the fish
in the baking dish and carefully break 4 eggs into the dish.
Season with salt and cook until the eggs are baked. Season
lavishly with freshly ground black pepper and serve.

Roman glass
jug from Turriff,
Aberdeenshire,
about AD 100.

# STUFFED SMALL HERRINGS

The use of Worcester sauce may confuse you, but Audrey d'Arragonna of the Roman Cookery School used to make liquamen (the fermented fish sauce that the Romans ate with almost everything) according to a recipe from Apicius and you could barely distinguish it from Lee and Perrins. Pennyroyal is a herb that fell from favour in the last century.

If you don't have it replace it with mint but it was much used by the Romans and is the authentic flavour. The use of herrings in place of sardines in this recipe indicates that it originated in one of the Roman provinces that touched the Atlantic and may have been of British origin.

6 small herrings
Worcester sauce
salt
1/8 tsp each cumin and pennyroyal
(1 1/2 tsps mint can be used instead
of pennyroyal)
55g/2oz chopped almonds
1 tbsp honey

Open the herrings and remove the backbones, leaving the fish whole. Rub with salt. Mix together the herbs and spices and finely chopped almonds and bind with the honey. Fill the fish with the stuffing. Wrap in vine leaves or tinfoil. Place in a steamer over boiling water and steam gently for 20 minutes or until cooked. Serve with Worcester sauce.

Face-masks which formed
part of parade helmets worn
by Roman soldiers, Newstead
AD 80-100.

# Herring in the Fashion of Bute

The Stuarts of Bute have lived on their island off the west coast for over nine hundred years and they have always been a force in Scottish history. The last Earl of Bute, before the family was raised to a Marquisate, was Prime Minister of England under George III. This somewhat obscured the fact that he was one of the finest botanists of his day. He was not a very successful PM and it was said he obtained the post because of his great charm and the beauty of his legs. He was much beloved by the widowed mother of George III, Caroline, Princess of Wales. The Butes have always lived in some style, the 3rd Marquis, who was the richest man in Europe and a great builder, was responsible for the architectural wonder of Mount Stuart. This elegant recipe for the use of herrings is well worth the initial effort. The finest herrings, known as 'Glasgow Magistrates' because of their plumpness, were fished in Loch Fyne and the Kyles of Bute.

4 herrings
1/2 tsp salt
40g/1 1/2 oz sugar
300ml/1/2 pint cold water
150ml/1/4 pint white wine
juice of 1 lemon
450g/1 lb boiled new potatoes finely diced
2 hardboiled eggs chopped
handful each chopped parsley, and other green herbs as liked
1 tbsp capers, chopped

FOR GREEN DRESSING:

parsley, mint and thyme

olive oil

salt and pepper

sugar

Behead the fish, clean and remove bones leaving fish whole, lay on a flat dish and sprinkle with salt and sugar. Leave for 4 hours, drain and dry thoroughly. Loosely roll up herrings starting at the head, skin side out, and place in an ovenproof dish. Pour over water, wine and lemon juice and bake at 180C/350F/Gas 4 for 45 minutes. Remove from the oven, drain, cool and chill.

Mix together the eggs, potatoes and capers and herbs. Make a green dressing by mincing parsley, mint and thyme in the food processor. Add olive oil, salt, pepper and a pinch of sugar, mix with the potato mixture. Place mixture into the centre of each rolled up herring and serve.

The Bute mazer or drinking bowl, 14th century.

# COLLARED SALMON

This is another recipe for preserving salmon. It is from the late seventeenth century and the use of mace, cloves and cayenne is indicative of the time. The word 'collared' refers to the fact that the salmon is rolled up to resemble a collar. The fish keeps very well in the pickle and is very unusual.

1 salmon

salt and pepper

large pinch each cayenne, pepper and mace

600ml/1 pint water

150ml/5 fl oz white wine vinegar

12 peppercorns

2 cloves

1/2 tsp allspice

2 bay leaves

Clean the salmon and cut into two long fillets along the backbone, skin and remove any bones. Mix together the salt, pepper, cayenne and mace, and rub over both sides of both fillets. Roll up the fillets starting at the tail end and bind firmly with string. Bring the water and vinegar to the boil, add the peppercorns, allspice, bay leaves and salt to taste. Put in the fish and simmer very gently for 1 hour. When cooked place in a non-metal container and pour over the pickling liquid to cover, adding more vinegar if necessary. Keep for at least 24 hours before using. To serve, drain from the liquid and serve with anchovy sauce.

Spearing salmon at night with a leister, early 19th century.

# Matius' Ragout

I don't know who Matius was but his is one of the few Romano-British recipes that have come down to us. As he was based in York in the second century AD – around the time of the Antonine settlements – I like to imagine he did service in Scotland and perhaps even cooked this dish in the village of Inveresk where I live, once the site of a Roman garrison. Although the occupation of lowland Scotland did not last long in comparison to the domination of England, the Roman presence north of Hadrian's Wall and its later northern counterpart the Antonine Wall was far more extensive than is generally realised.

1 tbsp olive oil

300ml/1/2 pint stock

2 leeks

1 tbsp fresh coriander, chopped

small dumplings made of 225g/8oz raw minced pork and breadcrumbs bound with beaten egg

450g/l lb cooked ham, diced

2 sharp eating apples, peeled, cored and diced

FOR THE SAUCE:

black pepper

1/2 tsp each cumin and coriander seed

mint

pinch of rue

1 tbsp each wine vinegar and stock

1 tsp honey

Heat the oil in a pan and saute the leeks, fresh coriander and dumplings. Add stock and ham. Leave this to cook gently, covered, for 45 minutes, then add the diced apples and cook for 10 minutes more. Pound the spices in a mortar, transfer to a pan and add vinegar, stock, boiled wine and honey, add some sauce from the ragout. Add the spice mixture to the ragout. This was traditionally thickened by adding pieces of pastry but use a beurre manie. Sprinkle with pepper and serve.

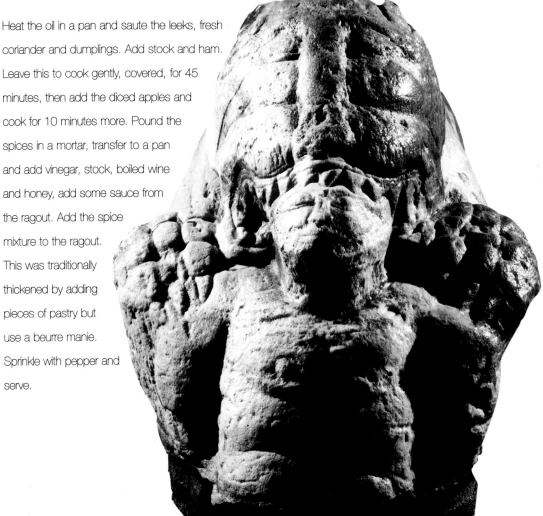

Sculpture of a lioness and her prey, found at Cramond, near Edinburgh, AD 140-250.

# Venison Pasty

Scottish cookery books contain a great many recipes for
venison. The red deer is native to Scotland and has been part
of the country's diet since, in the legal adage, 'time to which the
mind of man runneth not'. The punitive Norman game laws that
reserved venison for the nobility in England were never part of
Scottish law and as deer were a veritable pest, plundering the
crops in upland areas, the eating of them was encouraged. The
first haggis were almost certainly made from venison as the
sheep was a late comer to the Scottish scene.

This fine big venison pasty which would traditionally have been
decorated with scenes of hounds and deer would have proudly
graced any table. It makes me think of Burns' lines

*My heart's in the Highlands, my heart is not here*
*My heart's in the Highlands a chasing the deer.*
*A chasing the red deer, a following the roe,*
*My heart's in the Highlands wherever I go.*

900g/2 lb breast, flank or shoulder of venison
salt and pepper
55g/2oz flour seasoned with mustard and cayenne pepper
55g/2oz butter;
150ml/5 fl oz port
1 tsp wine vinegar
300ml/1/2 pint venison stock
pinch of thyme
1 tsp nutmeg
1 tbsp redcurrant jelly
150g/6oz fat bacon
565g/1 1/4 lb shortcrust pastry
beaten egg or milk to glaze

Cut the venison into flat pieces (collops), season and dust in seasoned flour. Melt the butter and fry the collops quickly to seal. Place in a 1.8 litre/3 pint pie dish and add the port, vinegar, redcurrant jelly, nutmeg and thyme. Cut the bacon into strips and lay on top. Roll out the pastry and cover the pie dish leaving a hole in the top to allow the steam to escape. Decorate with pastry trimmings. Glaze with milk or egg. Bake in a preheated oven at 220C/425F/Gas 7  for 15 minutes, reduce to 180C/350F/Gas 4 for a further 1 3/4 hours. Half an hour before the end of cooking add more stock through the hole in the top if necessary. Serve with mashed neeps and green cabbage or kail.

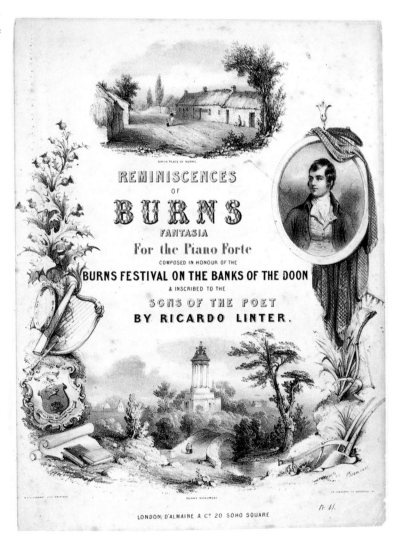

Sheet music cover for Reminiscences of Burns.

# Haunch of Venison

When I was a child one of my father's patients, the Earl of Caithness, used to send us a haunch of venison every year. He was in the far north and we were in London, and the haunch was simply contained in a rush bag with sprigs of bog myrtle to keep off the flies, and sent by train. If the weather was hot it was sometimes very ripe indeed when it arrived. I remember one year my mother buried it as it was inedible, to the delight of the dog who dug it up and ate it all over a rather good Persian rug. This is a traditional Scots way of cooking it and very good.

2.25kg/5 lb haunch of venison
salt, pepper and mixed spice
600ml/1 pint claret
juice of 3 lemons
275g/10 oz butter
flour
300ml/ 1/2 pint venison stock
1tsp walnut ketchup

Rub the haunch well with salt, pepper and mixed spice. Marinate in the claret and lemon juice for 6 hours, basting frequently. Place in a roasting pan with 150g/6oz melted butter, pour the marinade over the venison and cover with foil. Roast at a high heat 220C/425F/Gas 7 for 20 minutes to seal the meat, then reduce to 180C/350F/Gas 4 and continue roasting for 15 minutes per 450g/1lb. Remove the foil, cover the haunch with the remaining butter and dredge with flour. Cook for a further 15 minutes. Remove to a serving dish and keep warm. Add the stock to the pan juices and boil up, skim and season with walnut ketchup. Serve with the roast.

Spurs and hunting horn of Wat o' Harden, a Borders reiver. It is said his wife would serve the spurs on a plate to remind him to go cattle stealing.

# BEEF CECILS

This is an eighteenth-century dish and, whilst the Cecil family
was of course a famous English house, it is a dish which I keep
coming across in Scots books of the period. In eighteenth-
century kitchens the cook always kept a barrel of anchovies
and pickled walnuts were also a flavour of the age. Walnut trees
grow well in Scotland but, due to the climate, the nuts seldom
ripen; they are however perfect for pickling. Any visit to
Edinburgh is incomplete without a visit to the perfect eighteenth-
century kitchen of the Georgian House in Charlotte Square - I
cannot enter it without mentally rolling up my sleeves and
preparing to cook and I can visualise this dish being prepared
there. Remember it was not until the invention of the metal
grinder in Victorian times that meat was minced rather than
finely chopped.

4 slices cooked beef
1 large onion
2 anchovies
handful of parsley
salt and pepper
walnut pickle
cup of white breadcrumbs
flour

FOR THE GRAVY:

onions

beef stock

red wine

orange marmalade

Chop the cooked beef finely and mix with the breadcrumbs, finely chopped onion and chopped anchovy, parsley, pepper and salt and walnut pickle. Melt a little butter in a pan and heat this mixture gently. When cold enough to handle, form into large oval balls, mixing in a little flour to help it cohere. Roll the balls first in egg, then in breadcrumbs. Grill until cooked and serve with onion gravy. For the gravy fry up thinly sliced onions in oil, add beef stock, red wine and a spoonful of orange marmalade.

Bull on Pictish symbol stone from Burghead, Moray, 7th-8th century AD.

# OYSTER LOAVES

Edinburgh was famous for its oyster bars, indeed claret and oysters were the taste of seventeenth-century Edinburgh. In this simple dish we can see the origin of the Cajun 'pooboys' so beloved of Louisiana. Oysters are once again a major Scottish export thanks to my friend Johnny Noble of Loch Fyne. When Johnny inherited he told the Bank that among other ventures he wanted to develop an oyster bed. 'Well', they replied in the perspicacious manner of bankers, 'everyone should have a hobby'. His oysters are now exported all over the world! He tells me he knew there had been an oyster bed there because his war work as a boy was grinding up oyster shells collected on the shore for the chickens. The majority of oysters raised in Scotland are now the Portuguese strain but I was recently bought some wild natives from a bed on the far side of Skye which is only accessible during the equinoctial tides - they were seriously wonderful.

4 morning rolls
115g/4oz butter melted
12 fresh oysters
2 tbsp white wine
pinch nutmeg
pinch mace

Carefully remove the tops of the rolls and scoop out the crumb. Brush the insides of the rolls and the lids with melted butter. Place the rolls in a hot oven (220C/425F/Gas 7) to warm through.
Saute the oysters in the butter for 2-3 minutes, add the wine, spices and oyster liquor to the pan. Divide the oysters among the rolls and serve.

Commemorative Robert Burns decanter, whisky glass and a bottle.

# Leg of Mutton with Lemons

The Scots were particularly fussy about mutton in the Age of
Enlightenment and no self-respecting trencherman would eat
anything from a beast of less than four years old. If you
remember that sheep were largely reared for their wool, one
needed to find the balance between producing a prime wool
crop and eating a prime beast. To shear your beast in its
second, third and fourth year when the wool is at its best and
then slaughter it is sound commercial sense. This Georgian
dish is very good and must have been rather flashy as lemons
were still expensive. You can buy mutton in a Halal butcher or
from specialist suppliers.

900g/2lb mutton or lamb

3 lemons

300ml/ 1/2 pint stock

85g/3oz currants

1 tbsp peppercorns coarsely crushed

1tsp white wine vinegar

1tbsp sugar

Put the mutton in a closely covered saucepan with the stock
and simmer for 45 minutes, remove and cut into pieces. Return
to the pan with the lemons, thinly sliced, the currants, sugar
and the pepper. Cook for another 45 minutes, add the vinegar
and serve with sippets of toast.

Hand-clipping a sheep on the island of Flotta in Orkney in 1924. Scottish Life Archive

# Mince and Tatties

If a Scotsman wishes to describe himself as a plain man, he says 'I'm a mince and tatties man myself.'

Mince and tatties has kept a nation fed and healthy down the centuries. It is real comfort food, and, I suppose, the Scots variant of or possible inspiration for, the English cottage pie.

675g/1 1/2lb good beef mince

1 onion peeled but kept whole

salt and pepper

900g/2lb potatoes

55g/2oz strong cheese grated

1/4 pint beef stock or water

Fry the mince till brown, pouring away any fat. Put in a deep dish with the onion and season, add quarter pint beef stock or water cover and cook gently for about 1 hour. Boil and mash your potatoes, season well, put in a separate dish and sprinkle cheese on top. Brown in the oven or under a grill until the cheese is melted and bubbling. In order to enliven this simple dish you can add whatever you like to the mince, but this is it in its purity.

Cattle relaxing on the fringe of the
Great Cockle Shore – also the Isle of
Barra's airport. Alasdair Alpin
MacGregor, Scottish Life Archive

# Stoved Howtowdie wi' drappit eggs

900g/2lb chicken

salt and freshly ground black pepper

55g/2oz butter

225g/8oz shallots, chopped

a faggot of herbs

450ml/ 3/4 pint good chicken stock

4 eggs

FOR HERB FORCEMEAT:

1-2 onions, finely chopped

1-2 cloves garlic, crushed

butter

225g/8oz fresh breadcrumbs

lots of fresh green herbs, chopped

Season the chicken inside and out. Make the forcemeat by softening the onions and garlic in butter, adding the breadcrumbs and herbs and frying gently until golden. Stuff the chicken with forcemeat. Melt the butter in a casserole and brown the chicken all over. Add the shallots, faggot of herbs and rosemary. Pour the stock over the top. Cover tightly and simmer for 1 hour until the chicken is tender. Remove the chicken from the stock and keep warm. Ladle some of the stock into another pan and poach the eggs in it. To serve place flattened balls of kale on a flat serving dish, place the poached eggs on top of these and place the chicken in the middle.

An advertisement for hen feed, from Greenock, Renfrewshire. Scottish Life Archive

# Drappit eggs wi' cases

This is a delightful and elegant eighteenth-century supper dish but it is also very good for a starter or a light lunch. The pastry for the cases is very short indeed and can be used for cheese straws.

85g/3oz butter
85g/3oz strong cheddar-type cheese
85g/3oz flour
pinch salt
pinch mustard

Mix all the ingredients together until they form a stiff paste, a food processor is best for this.Wrap and chill for at least one hour, this will happily keep for several days in the fridge. Roll out the pastry to 2.5cm/1 inch thickness and cut with a large scone cutter. Bake in a hot oven (200C/400F/Gas6) for 10 minutes or until golden brown.

1/2 pint double cream
juice of 1 orange and 1 lemon
bunch flat-leaved parsley
bunch spring onions
1 egg per person

Mix together the cream and the fruit juices. Chop the parsley and spring onions and mix together. Spread some parsley mixture on each case and trickle over a little mixed cream. Poach your eggs, drain well and place on each case. Pour on a little more sauce and serve.

Feeding the poultry in the 1890s. Scottish Life Archive

## Haggis

As the author of a serious book on the haggis I can assure you that there is not enough space to extol the virtues and history of Scotland's national dish. The first haggis was almost undoubtedly made from venison as the sheep was an unwelcome latecomer to the Highlands, and John Macsween, the Edinburgh haggis maker of Skye descent, says that you can trace the progress of the haggis from northwest Scotland spreading downwards and across. Other nations have produced their own variant of this dish and it is undoubtedly Robert Burns who, in immortalising the haggis in his powerful political paean to the common man, has identified it so firmly with Scotland. This recipe includes fruit, which one often finds in old haggis recipes, but is not much used today. I like it however. Walter Scott in his St Ronan's Well gives some extraordinary recipes for haggis adding cockscombs and deer's tongues. The introduction of the Swedish turnip by Peter Miller of Dalswinton in the eighteenth century revolutionised farming methods. Arriving as it did at much the same time as the potato it gave rise to neeps and tatties or clapshot, now traditionally eaten with haggis.

Take a sheep's paunch and pluck, some of the lungs, liver and heart and sometimes the kidneys. Take the suet from round the kidneys and chop it finely. Add a pint of medium oatmeal, a good amount of chopped onion, 1 tbsp salt, dash black pepper, half a nutmeg, a handful of currants, raisins or any available fruit element. Mix well and pack into the paunch. The secret of making a good haggis is to allow for the swelling up of the meal to fill the elastic stomach tightly without bursting. It may be necessary to prick the haggis slightly when the boiling is beginning to let out air. It is easier to sew it up though the correct fashion is to wrap the stomach over using wooden skewers. Simmer for 4 hours.

## Clapshot

Peel two pounds of old potatoes and the same of swedes, cut into equal size pieces and boil together until they are soft. Drain and allow to stand until they have stopped steaming and are dry. Return to the pan and mash well together, stand over a low heat to dry them further, then add a good knob of butter and salt and pepper, mix well in, add some double cream and heat through. This is good transferred to a serving dish, dotted with butter and allowed to brown.

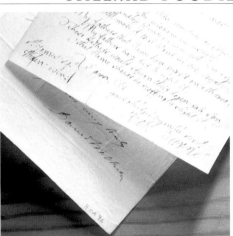

Letter from Robert Burns, 1788.

## Haggis and Beetroot in Puff Pastry

To show that haggis continues as a modern dish I give you this dish which I invented as a starter for a charity dinner given by James Thompson at the Witchery by the Castle.

1 haggis

1 jar sweet pickled beetroot

450g/1 lb puff pastry

salt and pepper

1 egg·

Illustration from Robert Burns' Tam o'Shanter, by John Faed.

Roll out your puff pastry and cut into 4 squares. On each square lay a helping of haggis and several slices of beetroot. Season well. Fold over and seal with the beaten egg. Glaze with egg and bake in a hot oven until the pastry is golden brown.

# Green Kail

The old Highland expression for have you eaten was 'have ye had kail'. This rather tough green brassica flourished in Scotland and provided the staple green supplement to the native diet. Kail is very high in iron but is a difficult vegetable to present attractively. This is a traditional and rustic preparation, and interestingly the use of cream in a peasant dish shows the commonplace use of cream in cooking at all levels, a habit which did not transfer to England till the arrival there of James VI.

900g/2lb kail
2 tbsp oatmeal
pepper and salt
2 tbsp double cream

Put enough water to cover the greens into a pot and bring to the boil. Remove the tough stalks from the kail and put the rest into the boiling water, simmer for an hour uncovered. Drain and squeeze out all moisture. Chop finely. Put back in the pot and sprinkle on the oatmeal, add the cream, salt and pepper. Heat through and serve with thin oatcakes.

Brian Stewart Wilson of Fair Isle, Shetland, in
1956, carrying a bunch of kail. Alasdair Alpin
MacGregor, Scottish Life Archive

# CROWDIE POTATO CAKES

The potato came late to Scotland. It was anathematised by the
Ministers of the Kirk because it was not mentioned in the Bible,
and a splendid story is told of the islanders of Skye who, forced
to plant them by the Macdonald of the day, harvested their
whole crop and dumped them on his doorstep saying 'Ye can
make us grow them but ye canna force us to the sin of eating
them'. However once they became established they took off
with a vengeance. Crowdie is the native Scottish curd cheese.

450g/1lb hot mashed potatoes
1 egg yolk
55g/2oz crowdie cheese
85-115g/3-4oz butter
1 tbsp chives chopped
salt and pepper

Mix the egg yolks and cheese into the hot potatoes with
55g/2oz butter, the chives and salt and pepper. Shape into
small rounds 2cm/ 3/4 inch thick, and fry in hot butter until
golden brown on both sides.

Farmworkers with a fine haul of potatoes. Scottish Life Archive

# BUTTERED ORANGES

Very little credit is given to the Stewart kings for their love of beauty, music, the arts and good food. James VI perhaps suffers most. Great focus is placed on his physical and sexual peculiarities, ignoring the fact that he ruled a hostile Scotland for twenty odd years before handling the ascent of the English throne (and England was, remember, the old enemy) without a shot fired in anger. The man who gave us Inigo Jones also gave us this his favourite recipe. Sweet oranges were a novelty in the sixteenth century having only recently been discovered in Ceylon. In this dish the oranges are filled with the delicious mixture, the tops replaced and they are served in a basket as if au nature. One can envisage the cries of 'Oo oranges!' quickly followed by even greater delight at the surprise.

6 hollowed-out small orange shells

2 large juicy oranges

55g/2oz castor sugar

5 egg yolks

1 tsp rose water

115g/4oz soft unsalted butter cut into 2.5cm/1 inch cubes

150ml/ 1/4 pint double cream

1 large piece soft candied orange

Remove a lid at the end of the orange furthest from the stalk and remove the pith. Carefully hollow out the orange taking care not to pierce the skin. Grate the rind from the two oranges and squeeze their juice. Mix the rind, juice, egg yolks and sugar in a small basin and place over a pan of boiling water. Stir gently but continuously with a balloon whisk until the mixture is as thick as a good custard.

(Do not whisk too briskly and take care to scrape the sides of the bowl from time to time.) When the orange mixture starts to ribbon remove the basin and stand in cold water to cool slightly, still stirring add the rosewater. Remove from the cold water. Whisk the butter pieces into the mixture one at a time, making sure each one is incorporated before adding the next. Half whip the cream and fold into the mixture. Cut the candied orange into tiny pieces, and as the mixture starts to set fold these in so that they stay suspended and do not sink to the bottom. Fill the orange shells with the mixture and replace the lids, put in a napkin-lined basket and serve.

James VI. Artist unknown

# Mary, Queen of Scots' Bombe

Although French influences in Scots cookery had been around
for some time, French cookery itself didn't actually improve
dramatically until the advent of the Medicis. Mary's mother in law
was of course Catherine de Medici and so Mary was exposed
to the first and possibly finest influence of this flowering.
Catherine was both a glutton and a gourmet, her constant
snack being artichoke hearts stuffed with cockscombs. The
novelty of iced food and drinks was introduced into France at
this point and it was far easier for Mary to obtain access to ice
and snow in her native Scotland. Little was understood of the
chemical reaction of sugar when frozen, so most glaces were
semi-liquid. However we do have a strange recipe which
combined a traditional egg and cream base sweetened with
Malmsey frozen into a bombe and filled with fresh fruit and then
frozen. Whilst much controversy still reigns as to whether Mary
engineered the explosion that killed her husband Darnley this is
one bombe she was responsible for!

Remember that fortified wine reduces the freezing temperature
by 0.6° F -1.2°F per 1 tbsp added to 1 litre/32fl oz mix.

350ml/12 fl oz milk

100g/3 1/2 oz soft light brown sugar

3 egg yolks

175ml/6 fl oz whipping cream (36% fat)

1 tbsp Malmsey wine

assortment raspberries, nectarines, peeled grapes,
apricots, cherries

Put the milk and half the sugar in a saucepan and heat to just
below boiling point. Remove from the heat. Beat together the
eggs and the rest of the sugar to a ribbon consistency and
pour on the almost boiling milk, whisking steadily. Place over

a pan of simmering water and stir the custard until it thickens to coat the back of a spoon. Remove from heat and plunge into cold water. Allow to cool completely and refrigerate. Stir in the Malmsey. Churn or stir freeze. Line the bombe mould with the ice-cream mix and freeze hard. Fill with an assortment of fruit, close the mould and freeze. When the bombe is cut the fruit tumbles out charmingly.

Gold enamelled locket set with onyx cameo portrait of Mary, Queen of Scots.

# CLARET JELLY

Claret was very much the drink of Scotland - indeed there is a verse which rails against the corruptive English influence in the eighteenth century that encouraged the Scots to drink port and so sap their natural vitality. This is a very grown up jelly, it looks wonderful and repays using a complex jelly mould. Don't do what I once did for a demonstration in Edinburgh where I was so afraid my jelly wouldn't turn out that I added an extra leaf of gelatine. I turned over the jelly and there was a deathly hush - nothing dropped and it took me four tries to turn it out! One woman said it was the best bit of the demo.

5 leaves gelatine or 2 sachets powdered
1 bottle claret type wine
1/2 wineglass brandy
1 small jar redcurrant jelly
grated rind and juice of 1 orange
55g/2oz caster sugar

Soften the gelatine in a little cold water. Put all the remaining ingredients into a saucepan, bring to the boil and simmer for 10 minutes. Pour onto the gelatine, stirring well untiil it is completely dissolved (if using leaf gelatine drain it and add to the hot liquid off the heat). Allow to cool slightly, then pour into a wetted jelly mould. Chill until set. Turn out and serve.

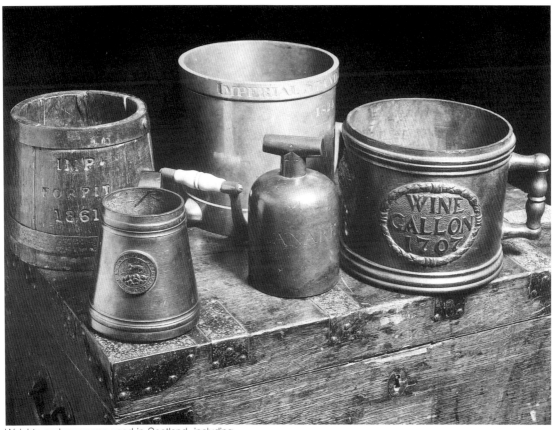

Weights and measures used in Scotland, including
a wine gallon dated 1707.

# Trinity House Creams

In the seventeenth century, when a young Scot by the name of John Reid went to Trinity College Cambridge as a tutor, he offered the kitchens his mother's recipe which they rather rudely rejected. On his ascension some years later to the faculty he served this recipe at his inaugural dinner. It has, due to the Victorian fascination with labelling dishes with French names, become famous in the world as creme brulee, though I have often, as a bookseller, had tearful French brides who did not recognise the dish their English husband demanded. Today's chefs brulee this dish with a blowtorch which more readily replicates the salamander used in earlier times. If using a conventional grill make sure the pudding is well chilled and the grill red hot before bruleeing it.

8 egg yolks

600ml/1 pint double cream

1 tsp cornflour

55g/2oz caster sugar

1/2 a vanilla pod

Cream the egg yolks, sugar and cornflour until they are quite white. Put the vanilla pod into the cream and bring to the boil over a low heat. Leave to stand off the heat for five minutes and remove the pod. Return the cream to the boil and pour directly onto the yolks whisking as you go. Place the basin over a pan of boiling water and slowly and gently stir the cream until it is quite thick and the whisk leaves a definite trail. As soon as it is thick stand it in cold water. Pour into the dish or dishes you intend to serve it in, allow to cool completely, then refrigerate for at least 6 hours. An hour before serving preheat the grill red hot and dredge the top of the creams with caster sugar. Place on a heatproof tray under the grill until the sugar has melted and caramelised. Set aside in a cool place (do not return to the refrigerator as this will soften the top).

Dairymaids in their striped aprons, milking a cow in the 1890s. Scottish Life Archive

# ⊙ATCAKES

Until well into the sixteenth century oats were the staple meal crop of Scotland. Even today relatively little wheat is grown here and oatmeal porridge and oatcakes have long been the foundations of the Scottish diet. Oatcakes have advantages over bread in that they are easily portable, light and last almost indefinitely. You can thicken a soup or stew with them and they lend themselves to any flavour. I am constantly impressed with how many people still make their own despite the plethora of commercially produced ones available.

225g/8oz fine oatmeal
1/2 tbsp fat
1/4 tsp salt
1/2 tsp bicarbonate of soda
warm water

Put the oatmeal, salt and bicarbonate in a bowl and work the fat into this, then add enough water to form a stiff but pliable dough. Roll out to an eighth of an inch thick. You may either cut this into a large round and quarter it or cut into small rounds. Heat on your girdle for 5 minutes turning once. For a crisper effect finish off in a hot oven for a few minutes more.

A meal break at the hairst,
near Auchendinny,
Midlothian. Artist unknown

# BARLEY BANNOCKS

Wheat did not grow north of the Highland line and Scotland's other staple crop was barley which was grown on the more fertile land available. Barley or bere meal has a very distinctive flavour and is still devoutly eaten in Orkney. It is to be found in health food shops and is a useful dietary addition for people with a wheat allergy. Whether the point of this verse is simply that Highlanders never ask for quarter in a fight (bruylie) or that the more prosperous warriors fed on the more expensive barley bannocks rather than the commoner oatcakes I leave to you.

*Wha in a bruylie, will first cry a parley,*
*never the lads wi' the bannocks o' barley!*
*bannocks of bere meal, bannocks of barley,*
*Here's to the Heiland Man's bannocks o' barley!*

generous 25g/1oz barley meal
300ml/1/2 pint milk
pinch of salt
25g/1oz butter

Bring to the boil the milk, salt and butter, and stir in enough barley meal to make a pliable dough. Turn onto a floured board, roll out thinly, handling as little as possible, and cut into large rounds. Bake on a hot girdle, turning once, and eat hot.

Tobacco shop sign,
late 18th century.

# BALMORAL DESSERT BISCUITS

Queen Victoria's love affair with Scotland is well known. No
doubt it was kindled by the Earl of Eglinton's splendid romantic
medieval tournament held to celebrate her coronation, where all
the aristocracy jousted in full armour for the young Queen's
favour. Therefore her affection existed long before she came to
Deeside with her beloved Albert or clapped eyes on the brawny
thews of John Brown, the piece of rough trade that so irritated
the Victorian Court. This recipe is from the archives at Balmoral
and produces a savoury biscuit that goes very well with our fine
Scottish cheeses.

225g/8oz flour
25g/1oz butter
4 egg yolks
2 egg whites

Mix all the ingredients into a stiff paste. Roll out very thin and
cut into round shapes the size of the top of a teacup with a
wavy edged pastry cutter. Bake in a slow oven. The biscuits
should be quite thin and blistered all over but not browned and
the blisters should be no darker than the whole.

The Eglinton Tournament, which was sadly spoiled by rain.

Balmoral tartan, designed by Prince Albert in the 1850s.

# Barley Meal Scones

These excellent scones come from Lady Clarke of Tillypronie's splendid book of recipes, collected by this redoubtable lady who lived on Deeside at the end of the nineteenth century. I once asked the late great Elizabeth David what was her favourite book and she chose from all her extensive library this work. I own ED's own copy today and it is a source of great pleasure to me. Lady Clarke describes these scones as 'thick as breakfast toast quite soft and mellow and tender inside'.

Take half a pound of barley meal flour and add to a pan of boiling water, add salt, lower the heat and cook like porridge very slowly, stirring continually. Cook for about 15 minutes.

Flour a board well with dry barley meal flour, the mixture must not be allowed to cool or it will get heavy. Take a spoonful of porridge and spread on the dry meal. Do not work it, just cover over with more barley meal flour, cut with a cutter and place onto the hot girdle at once. Cook on the girdle turning once and wrap in a linen napkin and keep warm. If they cool they become tough.

Victorian carpet bowls.

# Treacle Drop Scones

The Scottish Food writer Marian Macneill says that if every
French woman is born with a saucepan in her hand every
Scots woman is born with a rolling pin in her hand, and certainly
the tradition of baking is strong in Scotland. It used to be the
test of a good daughter-in-law that she could bake a good
scone and these treacle scones make a good variation on the
theme.

115g/4oz self-raising flour
pinch of salt
2 level tsp brown sugar
2 tbsp black treacle
1 egg beaten
scant 150ml/ 1/4 pint milk

Sift the flour and salt into a bowl and mix in the sugar. Heat the
treacle gently, till it flows, then add to the dry ingredients with
the egg and half the milk. Beat until smooth, gradually adding
the remaining milk. Heat the griddle or a heavy frying pan and
rub lightly with oil. Drop dessertspoonfuls of batter onto the
griddle and cook for 3-4 minutes until bubbles rise to the
surface and the undersides are lightly browned. Turn over and
continue for 2-3 minutes until lightly browned. Remove to a
clean towel and wrap to keep warm while cooking the rest.
Spread with butter and serve.

Shortbread mould, advertising Brown & Polson's 'Paisley Flour.'

# FRED MACKENZIE'S SCONES

I imagine it was the early advent of coal in Scotland that gave
us the edge on baking. The heat in a coal oven is much more
consistently reliable than that in a wood-burning one. Whilst
every Scots woman is required to bake a good scone, curiously
our scones at Lennoxlove are the province of my second chef
Fred Mackenzie. Fred, a dashing Highlander, whose mother
was an acting clan chief and who thinks nothing of staying up
all night during functions, trained as he is on the Northern
gathering and the Skye Balls, produces a great many flawless
scones and this is his recipe.

675g/1 1/2 lbs self raising flour
2 tsp baking powder
115g/4oz butter
115g/4oz sugar
2 eggs
pinch salt
approximately 300ml/ 1/2 pint milk

Sift flour, baking powder and salt; cut in butter and rub in well.
Mix together the eggs and the sugar and stir into the mixture
adding enough milk to make a stiff dough. Roll out to an inch
thick and cut into rounds with a cutter. Put onto a baking sheet
and bake at 400 for 12 minutes or until golden brown.

Silver tea set made for the Earl of Hopetoun, by James Ker, Edinburgh, 1734-5.

# Fochabers Gingerbread

Why Fochabers should have become particularly associated with this good rich gingerbread is beyond me, suffice it to say that there is a strong tradition of ginger in Scots cooking. Scotland had strong trade ties with 'La Serenissima', the mighty Venetian trading empire in the fifteenth century, which held a virtual monopoly on the spice trade until the late seventeenth century. The Stewart kings didn't have the land-rich power base that their English cousins possessed and were constantly surrounded by warring nobles whose claim to the throne was probably as good as theirs. In order to pay off these rivals they became 'Trader Kings', even, in the case of James III, marrying into the powerful trading empire of Flanders.

225g/8oz butter

115g/4oz caster sugar

225g/8oz black treacle

600ml/1 pint beer

450g/1 lb plain flour

1/2 tsp bicarbonate of soda

2 tsp each ground ginger and mixed spice

1tsp each ground cinnamon and cloves

115g/4oz each sultanas and currants

85g/3oz finely chopped peel

85g/3oz ground almonds

Line, grease and flour a round 25cm/10 inch cake tin. Cream the butter and sugar until pale and fluffy. Dissolve the treacle and the bicarbonate in the beer and sift in the spices. Fold alternately the flour and the treacle into the butter and sugar mixture. Add the fruit and the almonds. Pour into the tin and bake for 3 hours, at 180C/350F/Gas 4.

Wemyss ware plate, by Robert Heron's Fife Pottery,
Kirkcaldy, late 19th century.

# Marmalade

There is an old and charming story that tells that Mary Queen of Scots fell into a decline on her return to Scotland as a result of the dour weather and that her chef, in an effort to cheer her, created this orange jam reminiscent of the warmth and sweetness of the France she loved and that the name is based on his cry 'Madame est malade'. I have always loved that story but I fear it is untrue as the Ottoman Turks had been producing an orange jam called Marmelo for years. Marmalade really came into its own when William Keiller, a merchant of Dundee, received a shipment of Seville oranges by mistake in 1786 and persuaded his wife to convert them into Dundee Marmalade. This sold so well that he ordered more oranges. Today the entire Seville orange crop is sold to the British marmalade market. Food writers, and I am no exception in this, fear giving marmalade recipes as everyone has their own carefully prized one. This recipe is a straightforward one and please do not think I am setting myself up as any authority.

900g/2lb bitter oranges

2 lemons

1.8 litres/3pints water to 450g/1lb fruit

450g/1lb sugar to 600ml/1 pint pulp

Wash and weigh the fruit, carefully peel it, leaving the pith, measure the water and put in a bowl. Put the flesh and the juice of the fruit in the bowl with the water, tie the pips in a muslin bag, shred the peel and add everything to the measured water. Leave to soak overnight to soften the peel. Place the contents of the bowl in a preserving pan and bring to the boil. Cook until tender and until the liquid has reduced by half, about 1 hour. Measure the liquid pulp and allow 1 lb sugar to 1 pint pulp. Bring to the boil, stir in the sugar, dissolve and boil rapidly.

Test for setting either with a thermometer (a set will be obtained between 200-220 °F) or by the saucer method. Put a little jam on a cold saucer and allow to cool. Push a finger across the top of the jam, the surface will wrinkle when a set has been obtained. Allow to cool, stirring occasionally to prevent the fruit from rising to the top. Pot in clean warm jars, filling them to the top. Cover with a waxed disc and a damped cellophane cover secured with a rubber band.

The Penicuik Jewels, including a gold enamelled locket, a gold necklace and pendant said to have been a gift from Mary, Queen of Scots to her servant Giles Mowbray.

# Black Bun

Every Hogmanay the bringer of good luck for the coming year is the tall dark stranger carrying a lump of coal. He first foots across the threshold and is offered a dram (of whisky) and a slice of black bun.

225g/8 oz shortcrust pastry
450g/1 lb each raisins and currants
55g/2oz chopped mixed peel
115g/4oz blanched chopped almonds
115g/4oz soft brown sugar
225g/8oz plain flour

1 level tsp each ground cinnamon, ground ginger, ground allspice, cream of tartar, bicarbonate of soda
1 egg, beaten, and egg to glaze
150ml/ 1/4 pint whisky
4 tbsp milk

Grease an 20cm/8 inch round cake tin and line with greaseproof paper. Roll out the pastry and carefully line the tin keeping enough for a lid. Mix together the fruits, peel, almonds and sugar in a bowl. Sift the flour with the spices, cream of tartar and bicarbonate and mix evenly with the fruit. Add the egg and whisky and enough milk to just moisten the mixture. Pack the mixture into the pastry case. Roll out the remaining pastry to make a lid, brush the edges with egg to seal and press down firmly. Trim and crimp the edges and brush the top with egg. Make 6 or 8 holes right through the cake to the base with a skewer and prick the lid all over with a fork. Glaze again and bake in a moderate oven (180C/350F/Gas 4) for 2 1/2 to 3 hours covering the top with greaseproof paper when sufficiently browned. Cool in the tin for at least 30 minutes before turning out on a wire rack. Store in an airtight container or well wrapped in foil in a cool place for up to 6 months.

Water jug advertising whisky made by Pattison's, an Edinburgh distiller.

# ABERDEEN BUTTERIES (ROWIES)

This recipe was given to me by Kay, the present Duchess of
Hamilton, and a native Aberdonian. She tells me that one of the
features of baking in the town are these morning 'rowies' and
that the best ones are produced by Aitkens Bakery at
Glenbervie Road, Torry. This recipe was her mother's, and as
she says, 'heaven knows where it came from before that.'

400g/14oz plain flour
25g/1oz yeast
lukewarm water
115g/4oz lard
2 tsp salt
3 tsp sugar
butter

Sift flour into a warmed basin. Cream sugar and yeast in a cup
and mix with a little warm water. Pour onto flour and mix well
adding sufficient warm water to form a rather firm dough. Cover
and leave in a warm place for 45 minutes. Roll out, sprinkle on
the salt, then place lard onto the dough in walnut-sized pieces
and fold as for puff pastry. Roll out (not too thinly), cut into small
squares and turn in the corners. Cover and leave to rise for a
further 45 minutes. Put a knob of butter on each buttery and
bake for approximately 20 minutes at 230C/450F/Gas 8 until
lightly browned.

Milk churn, milking stool
and other dairy equipment.

# DUNDEE CAKE

Sue Lawrence, the greatest cook ever to come out of Dundee,
says that this cake is not really eaten in the town that bears its
name. It is, however, a cake much associated with the great
tradition of Scottish High Tea and is quite delicious.

150g/6oz unsalted butter, softened
150g/6oz caster sugar
grated zest of 1 orange
4 eggs
55g/2oz ground almonds
150g/6oz plain flour
1 tsp baking powder
1 tsp mixed spice
115g/4oz sultanas
115g/4oz raisins
115g/4oz currants
55g/2oz mixed peel
1 tbsp brandy
16 whole blanched almonds

Preheat the oven to 180C/300F/Gas 2. Cream together the
butter, sugar and orange zest until light and fluffy, then beat in
the eggs one at a time. Add a little of the flour if the mixture
starts to curdle.
Sift in the flour, baking powder and spice then add the ground
almonds. Fold gently but thoroughly. Once everything is
incorporated stir in the dried fruits and mixed peel, together with
enough brandy to form a soft consistency. Spoon into a
buttered lined 18cm/ 7 inch cake tin and smooth the top. Bake
in the oven for 2 1/2 to 3 hours or until cooked through.
Halfway through baking arrange the almonds on top and return
to the oven. Cool completely in the tin before serving.

Silver tea set by R&W Sorley, Glasgow, 1892.

# Parlies

These ginger cakes are so named because they were beloved by the members of the original Scots Parliament. I hope they will see a revival in the new one. I once promised to serve them to the new members, but they'll have to give us back beef on the bone first!

900g/2lb flour
450g/1lb brown sugar
115g/4oz ground ginger
450g/1lb unsalted butter
450g/1lb treacle
1 tsp black pepper

Mix together the flour, sugar and ginger. Melt the butter and add the treacle, pour this mixture onto the flour. Mix into a paste and as soon as it is just cool enough to handle roll into large cakes 0.5cm/1/6 inch thick or less. Mark in squares with a knife and cook at 160C/325F/Gas 3. Separate the squares whilst they are still warm and allow to cool.

Downsitting of Parliament, about 1680.

# Deep Fried Mars Bar

Scotland has long had a love affair with the frying pan and it is joked that they will deep fry anything. This was proved partly true by the advent of the deep fried Mars Bar. Sue Lawrence, eager to try it for her column in the Sunday Times, went into a chippie and ordered one. She was asked if she wanted it with chips, and when she declined she was asked 'salt n sauce?' which is how Edinburghers eat their fish and chips – with salt and brown sauce. It is, however, surprisingly good straight with ice cream.

Take a Mars bar and put it in the fridge for an hour. Remove the wrapper and dip it in batter. Deep fry it until the batter is crisp and golden and serve at once.

# Index